# 10 PHILOSOPHY OF RELIGION

## REVELATION, INSPIRATION AND SACRED WRITINGS

BY
PETER MANNING

First published 2004

Abacus Educational Services,
20 Malvern Close,
Worthing,
West Sussex,
BN11 2HE.

ISBN: 1 898653 27 5

Other titles available in the series:

1. Religious Language
2. The Problem of Evil
3. Faith and Reason
4. God and Proof
5. Revelation and Religious Experience
6. Life after Death
7. Miracles
8. Science and Religion
9. Freewill and Determinism (in preparation)

Also available:

Ethics series:

1. Ethical Theory and Language
2. Moral Laws
3. Christian Ethics
4. Homosexuality
5. Abortion
6. Euthanasia
7. Environmental Ethics
8. Business Ethics (in preparation)

Titles on the Fourth Gospel are also available.

# CONTENTS

# INTRODUCTION

This booklet has been written specifically to meet the needs of A/AS students of Religious Studies and General Studies. However, it may equally be used as an introduction to the debate over the role of revelation as a source of religious authority by the interested lay person or by first year undergraduates.

The booklet considers the possibility of revelation and how understandings of revelation vary across Semitic and Indian religious traditions. An engagement with comparative, historical and theological issues is sought at differing points in the text. With each religious tradition containing a great degree of diversity in belief and practice, it has been necessary to make simplifications less the text become over long. But hopefully there is enough here to inspire the reader to dig deeper into the riches and wonders of religious discourse and the various religions.

The style of the booklet is similar to that employed in other booklets in the Philosophy of Religion series produced by ABACUS. It is structured around key questions that have developed out of classroom experience. It also contains a section that deals with exam questions and should therefore be useful for both teaching and revision.

Further booklets in this series are being produced.

# WHAT IS RELIGION

## THE RELIGIOUS EXPERIENCE OF HUMANITY

We live in a world surrounded by religious ideas, rituals and symbols. Many of our towns and cities possess places of worship of various faiths. Religious rites of passage are often used to mark important life events such as birth, marriage and death. For some, religious devotion and membership of a faith community becomes the foundation stone around which their lives are lived. For others, religion is only engaged with, if at all, when life events occur which seem to need some kind of sacramental, holy or symbolic covering which purely secular forms of life inadequately provide. Perhaps such a need is driven by a desire to make sense of our lives by relating it to some kind of big picture, story about reality, which enables us to make sense of life.

The different religions, in their various ways, seek to address three key ultimate questions. Firstly there is a concern with the nature of ultimate reality, the most basic thing that exists and which underwrites the existence of everything else. Secondly, there is a concern to relate our understanding of what we are as human beings to that ultimate reality. Thirdly, in answer to the first two questions the means by which salvation, enlightenment or self-fulfilment may be obtained is identified. In addressing such questions the various religious traditions provide a story, a way of understanding reality and our place within it, which can give life a depth of focus and meaning perhaps not found outside of religious forms of life.

Religion or the yearning for some kind of spiritual foundation for life seems to be a universal human phenomena that has existed throughout the ages, from primal religions specific to a particular tribe and place, to canonical religions. Canonical religions can be divided into two main groups, Semitic and Indian religions. The Semitic religions of Judaism, Christianity and Islam all have a common heritage in the patriarch Abraham and trace their historical origins to the Middle East. The Indian religions of Hinduism, Buddhism and Sikhism have their historical origins in the Indian sub-continent. Canonical religions, because they possess a recognised sacred body of literature, are able to transcend the limits of both time and place and become principal religions of the world. Adherents of each of these religions are now found within most countries around the globe. Indeed in terms of the global population it is estimated that 33%, 1,833,022,000, of people identify with the Christian religion while another 18%, 971,328,700, align themselves with Islam. The majority of people alive in the world today follow a commitment to some kind of belief in God.

Even within the more secular western world of today, centred as it is on science and consumerism, a concern for the some kind of spiritual essence to life persists. Research conducted by the Alistair Hardy Research Centre based in Oxford under the guidance of David Hay found from national poll data collected in the United States, Britain and Australia that during the 1970s and 1980s 27% of people claimed an awareness of the presence of God, while 38% of those who had had such an experience had not told anyone else about the experience.

Given the persistence of claims to some kind of religious experience and the continuing impact of religion upon the lives of so many people world-wide what are we to make of the various religions and their claims to act as authorities on the ultimate questions of life? Are they to be seen as gatekeepers to the truth of reality or as something else? How is religion to be understood and defined? Such a question is key to approaching issues involved in revelation and religious authority.

## PROBLEMS IN DEFINING RELIGION

In attempting to study religion sociologists, who study human society, have attempted to understand the social organisation and social consequences of religious belief and practice. Commonly two definitions of religion have been used, the first termed 'functional' and the second called 'substantive'.

The first, a functional definition of religion, seeks to categorise the main functions of religion and show how these contribute to the maintenance of society. Religion is understood by what it *does*, the role or purpose it fulfils in the life of a community of believers. Hence, religion helps the community deal with ultimate problems, such as death, by explaining why people die or suffer. Bronislaw Malinowski (1884-1942) pioneered such an approach. He saw religion as the tool used by human communities to bind their experiences of the mysteries of life together and in so doing convey meaning to life and order to society. Through religious beliefs and practices the community found the means to legislate what were accepted and unaccepted patterns of behaviour. Such a definition may be termed anthropological because it seeks to define religion by focusing on human beings and what they do and say rather than focusing on God or some notion of a transcendent world. As a consequence functional definitions of religion don't just define religion but provide a theory of what religion is. For it is held that religion is best understood through a naturalistic view of the world which discounts any talk of the possible reality of God or the transcendent.

The second approach, a substantive definition of religion, focuses on what religion *is* by seeking to categorise the key features of religion and to discern what the religion itself gives significance to. Using such an approach it has commonly been understood that religion is concerned with belief in some kind of spiritual reality, involvement with supernatural powers and some kind of belief in God or gods. Such a substantive definition is concerned with how beliefs and practices relate the community to that which it affirms as sacred.

An extension of such a substantive approach which also contains elements of the functional definition of religion is that of Ninian Smart (1927-2001). This approach is often called the phenomenological approach to religion because it focuses on interpreting and categorising what it identifies as universal features of observed phenomena across the different religious traditions. Smart sought to identify and classify the main characteristics found within all religious traditions. He identified six universal features of religion which he called the dimensions of ritual, mythological, doctrinal, ethical, social, and the experiential. Ritual involves prayer, meditiation and other activities which seek to bring the individual closer to that which is taken to be the spiritual essence of life. The mythical dimension provides a narrative or story through which spiritual truth may be discerned. Doctrine provides a systematic code of beliefs and teachings through which life and its connection to the spiritual realm might be understood. Ethical codes provide a common set of values that seek to bind the life of the community together and encourage acceptance of the spiritual and sacred. The social dimension involves a consideration of the way in which religion acts as the organising hub of the customs of the community. Lastly, the experiential dimension is concerned with the religious experience of individuals and what it feels like to be involved in a religion.

The study of religion through each of these definitions has highlighted the diversity of religious belief and practice at a time when the western world, which has seen an attachment to Christianity through much of the last 2000 years, has become much more a multi-cultural and multi-faith society. Members of different faith communities interact through their working and social lives on a day to day basis like never before. We live in a world with many sacred texts with each religious tradition offering a different view of the world. In such a situation, in which there are varying alleged sources of revelation offering access to spiritual realities authority within religion has become a contested issue. Given this it may seem appealing to adopt an anthropological, sociological or phenomenological definition of religion. However, such definitions as those discussed above tend to remove too far from view the possibility that a spiritual realm might in fact exist and in so doing threaten to miss the heart of what religion claims to be. To reduce religion to the interpretive criteria provided by such disciplines stands the risk of recreating religion in the image of those disciplines rather than assessing religion on its own terms. Instead of being tools, amongst others, which shed light on religion sociology, anthropology and psychology can quickly become *the* means by which religion is to be properly understood. To make such a claim is a bolder and more problematic move than is often recognised and the imposing of naturalistic explanations upon religion needs arguing for, rather than being assumed.

What a religion claims through its doctrines and religious experience might after all connect with spiritual realities that cannot be summed up by, or caught within the net of, scientific method or human reason and the use of logical thought. To describe something is not always the same as saying everything that could be said about it, for perhaps some things can only be shown or experienced for oneself before the truth of the matter may be known. As William James remarked toward the end of *The Varieties of Religious Experience* the difference between talk about religion and living it is akin to the difference between analysing a menu and actually eating a four-square meal.

Arguably to take religion seriously involves seeking to move beyond descriptions of what religion is or does to an engagement with the theological quest for truth (Semitic religions), or seeking personal unity of being with that which is ultimate (Indian religions). There is an attempt to glimpse something of the religion from the inside rather than imposing an external interpretive framework upon it which is alien to the religious tradition in question. Given that such a quest, albeit in very different ways, is a central aspect of most religions, it would seem that what is needed is an open ended definition which does not *prejudge* the possibility of some kind of spiritual reality or transcendent being existing or not-existing. The issue is further complicated by Buddhism, which although commonly understood as a religion, and possessing a profound spirituality, essentially rejects the importance of the existence of God. In his book *Understanding Religion* Eric Sharpe proposes a definition that holds that religion involves belief in …

> 'the actual existence of a supernatural, suprasensory order of being, and of the actual or potential interplay, through a network of sacred symbols, of that order of being with the world in which normal life is lived.'
>
> Eric Sharpe, *Understanding Religion* (London: Duckworth, 1983) p.48.

Such a definition accepts the validity for the believer of the importance of such symbols as, for example, the cross, as signifiers of deeper spiritual truths. It also respects the possibility that religious rituals such as Holy Communion in Christianity may allow access to the divine life. The definition guards against defining from the outset whether the 'supernatural, suprasensory order of being' is theistic or, as with Buddhism, monistic. Monism involves seeing the unity of everything that exists in the same ultimate essence without reference to God. That religion is characterised as involving belief in 'the actual existence of a supernatural, suprasensory order of being' does not affirm that the religious believer is actually right in such a belief. For, religion might just be a construct of human societies and humanity's need to give life order, purpose and significance in a world without any ultimate meaning. But then again, the critical quest for truth or unity of being might offer evidence in support of such religious beliefs. Given this possibility, how has religion sought to establish how God may be known and therefore affirm the authority of religion as the guide to living the good or spiritual life?

# IS REVELATION POSSIBLE?

## TOWARD A GENERAL THEOLOGY OF REVELATION

It is a commonplace of human experience that knowledge comes to us as our minds, with their thoughts and feelings, engage the world we indwell with our five senses. We constantly come to know and appreciate new things not reasoned about or experienced before. Given this it might seem that all knowledge requires revelation if we mean by revelation the disclosure of knowledge about something or someone otherwise unknown. Samuel Taylor Coleridge once remarked that 'all truth is a species of revelation'.

Humanity has made amazing technological advances and gains in knowledge that testify to our ability to get to grips with reality. Within the western world this has encouraged a tendency to see humans as rational beings who act as autonomous agents, who freely choose what to do and believe, when deciding what the truth or falsity of a matter is. Such a stress on our own self-sufficiency sustains a view of human enquiry as capable of being detached, objective and precisely analytical. Indeed, the placing of such stress on autonomous reason stems from the philosopher Kant (1724-1804) who in answer to the question 'what is enlightenment?' remarked that it involved 'man's emergence from his self-incurred immaturity.' It was a call to forego external authorities, such as that contained in religion, and to think for oneself and in so doing exhibit a willingness to trust to the validity of ones own reasoned engagement with the world. This put revelation and reason on the path to conflict. For revelation, if seen as a purely religious phenomenon, stands against reason, if reason is seen as being grounded in the autonomy and self-sufficiency of the individual. If such a division is accepted then there can ultimately be no meeting of the ways between secular tools of understanding religion (anthropology, sociology and psychology) and spiritual tools of understanding religion (the appeal to divine authority or sacred experience). One will always in the final analysis have to choose one or the other, theistic or atheistic tools of understanding what religion is. The choice as to which you choose to listen to most will almost certainly be influenced by the view of the world and its assumptions that you have already accepted.

Yet as has already been stated above there is a sense in which revelation is a universal phenomena of human experience and cannot therefore stand wholly in conflict to reason. As the experience of coming to know is exactly that, an experience, it highlights our embodiment in the world. We know the world and other people as we relate to them. As human beings we engage both thoughts and feelings which are themselves shaped by our experiences of the world about us, and thus we do not stand as completely autonomous agents apart from the world. Indeed, even our scientific knowledge relies on theories developed by individuals such as Newton, Darwin and Einstein whose ideas stand within an ongoing dialogue of revision by those within the scientific community. To live involves being embedded in relationships to things and people. There is a real sense in which all knowledge, because of its locatedness in relationships, is a form of personal revelation. If all knowledge is at depth personal, however well attested by scientific method, the witness of history or shared human testimony, then reason and revelation far from being in conflict are hand-maidens to each other. As reasoning, sentient beings, we are engaged in an ongoing relationship with the world which reveals itself to us as we attune our five senses and the faculties of human reason to the world and the tasks of life.

Far from living in a world in which revelation is the peculiar pursuit of religion our lives are transfigured by revelation. For, revelation is the vehicle through which life, quite literally, finds its sense and meaning. As all knowledge is dependent on being revealed in some way to us as personal agents acting in the world, knowledge is also mediated to us rather than accessed in a direct or unmediated way. In that knowledge depends on some kind of relationship between us and that which we are striving to know, the tools of knowing, e.g. our five senses, the scientific method and its apparatus, meditation etc, become the vehicles of revelation which bring greater understanding to us.

To talk in the above way of the reciprocal relationship between reason and revelation is to chart, what has been called by Colin Gunton in his book *A Brief Theology of Revelation* (1995), the foundations of a General Theology of Revelation. Stating the possibility of such a general theology of revelation goes some way to healing the split between reason and religion that is often felt within western culture today.

## REVELATION AS GENERAL AND SPECIFIC

Such a general theology of revelation as that articulated above is also able to contain within itself two more common ways through which the nature of revelation is understood. These are revelation as general and specific.

General revelation involves the witness of the natural world to the existence of God or that which is the 'supernatural, suprasensory order of being.' Such claims to general revelation have often been located within holy texts, for example in the Christian New Testament book of Romans chapter 1 verse 20, which declares that 'Ever since God created the world, his invisible qualities, both his eternal power and divine nature, have been clearly seen; they are perceived in the things that God has made.' Some theologians, for example within Christianity and Islam, have used reason as a tool to reflect on the nature of the world and, using philosophical arguments, argue from observations of the world to the existence of God. Such an undertaking is called Natural Theology and encompasses the various arguments for the existence of God such as the ontological, design and cosmological arguments including the Islamic Kalam tradition. Another strand of reasoning about general revelation instead of focusing on the witness of the world to the existence of God seeks to articulate a theology of nature. Such a theology of nature attempts to articulate the way in which the natural world relates to God as creator (Judaism, Christianity, Islam and Sikhism), or to the spiritual realities underlying the surface appearances of the natural order as we perceive it (Hinduism and Buddhism).

Specific revelation relates to the witness of personal experience, historical events, miracles, and the transforming life of particular holy individuals, such as Jesus or the Buddha. Sacred texts as vehicles of divine revelation can also be understood as specific revelation. As holy books grapple with the three ultimate questions of life, what is the nature of the universe, what does it mean to be a human being, how are we to make the most of life or fulfil our spiritual calling, claims to knowledge or enlightenment are made. Such claims rest on the authority given to such texts by the various religious traditions. Each of the religious traditions provides significance to insights gained through general revelation by reflecting on the collected wisdom of specific revelation. So, for example, the insight from general revelation that order within the universe points toward God as creator finds further explanation within Judaism and Christianity through appeal to the Genesis creation story. The meaning of general revelation is therefore heavily bound up with the interpretive lenses provided by specific revelation. Determining how specific revelation is gained therefore becomes important for any discussion of religious authority, resting as it often does, on claims to revealed truth or wisdom. This brings us to a discussion of how two contrasting views construe the impartation of revelation.

## REVELATION AS PROPOSITIONAL OR NON-PROPOSITIONAL

How revelation is conveyed has been an area of much theological debate. Within the study of theology, and the comparative study of world religions, there are two broad approaches to how revelation is gained. These are the propositional and non-propositional approach.

The propositional view is so called because it involves asserting propositions, making statements about the way things are. So, for example, to say 'its raining outside' is to assert a propositional statement about reality. Within the propositional view, revelation is thought of as providing *information* about the divine nature and will of God. The lives of historical figures like that of Jesus and Mohammed are taken to be vehicles through which the divine discloses itself through a particular historical place and time in a unique way. Propositional approaches to revelation place a heavy emphasis on the supernatural activity of God in enabling humanity to know about God. Claims to such supernatural and unique revelations of God often lead to exclusivism in religious belief. Exclusivism entails that the Truth of God and humanities place in the cosmos is especially made known in that religious tradition rather than any other. Exclusivism literally 'excludes' other possibilities as it gives special emphasis to one particular viewpoint over any other perspectives. Often claims to revealed truth are supported by appeals to the sacred text itself as the actual 'word of God'. So for example, within Christianity an appeal might be made to the New Testament book 2 Timothy chapter 3, verse 16 which states that 'All scripture is inspired by God and is useful for teaching the truth, rebuking error, correcting faults, and giving instruction for right living.' Within Islam the idea that God revealed the words of the Qur'an to Muhammad secures a similar status for the Qur'an as the word of God. The Qur'an is seen as the greatest form of revelation known as *tanzil*. This form of revelation is only ever used of the Qur'an and denotes its status as being the direct words of God communicated into the mind of Muhammad through the agency of the angel Gabriel. Thus, the Qur'an is not humanly inspired writings or inspired by God through the agency of human beings but is a record of the eternal words of God given to Muhammad, remembered perfectly by him and recited by the followers of Muhammad. Islam is thus clearly attached to a propositional view of revelation.

Claims to the unique authority of revelation may be further supported through appeal to general revelation whether through reason and its appeal to natural theology and the arguments for the existence of God, or through a theology of nature which argues that given the way the world is, it is the specific revelation provided within that tradition which enables us to make most sense of the world. Reason plays a subordinate role to revelation as faith trusts in the miraculous disclosure of the divine to humanity and in so doing presupposes both the existence of the divine and that the truths in question are in fact from God. Within such a context faith is characterised by intellectual assent to a set of revealed truths contained in propositional form in sacred books and creedal statements of belief. Within Christianity such cognitive assent to belief has often been denoted by the Latin term *fides*. Faith is affirmed through an act of the will.

Within the non-propositional view the idea that revelation is information about the divine gained through propositions is rejected. Instead spiritual truth or wisdom is centered on reflections upon spiritual *experience*. Such spiritual experience may be occasioned by the self-giving action of God, or through the enlightened apprehension of ultimate realities through meditation or other intense religious experiences. The self-giving action of God involves the divine making itself known to the world through significant revelatory events within human history and the living of each individual life. Under this view revelation is not so clearly differentiated from other religious ideas or experiences. This is because revelation is made up of both divine activity and human attempts to recognise and understand it. Thus, there is much more room for interpretation and ambiguity within this approach to revelation than one centered on propositions. Within the non-propositional view faith involves an attitude of personal trust and commitment to the ultimate reality experienced through revelatory events. Within Christianity such experiential assent to belief has often been denoted by the Latin term *fiducia.* The real key to understanding God or the ultimate reality is not creedal statements or even sacred texts but rather those experiences of the supernatural order of being which are acknowledged as authoritative by the religious community. Thus reason is subordinated to experience. Such an experiential basis for belief has little need for natural theology with its rational arguments as proofs for the existence of God. Arguments over the inspiration of scripture become less significant as holy texts become not the 'word of God' but rather a record of the thoughts and experiences of those who have sought or experienced God or the ultimate reality. In other words holy books are not in themselves revelation but rather witnesses to revelatory events and experiences. Non-propositional approaches to revelation and religious belief lead to a more inclusive attitude to other religions outside of ones own. Inclusivism entails that truth or enlightenment may be found in different ways through many of the principal world religions.

The possibility of specific and general revelation, alongside a clash of perspectives over the way in which revelation is gained, brings us to a consideration of how different religious traditions relate revelation to authority.

# HOW DO DIFFERENT RELIGIOUS TRADITIONS RELATE TO REVELATION

## THREE BROAD TRADITIONS OF RELIGION

For a believer within a particular faith community there invariably exists the conviction that the religious tradition to which they belong provides access to a 'revealed' truth or wisdom about reality. Although there exists an immense range of diversity in religious belief and practice across the religions it is possible to group recipients of divine revelation into three broad traditions. These are Primal religious traditions, Semitic religious traditions (Judaism, Christianity and Islam), and Indian religious traditions (Hinduism, Buddhism and Sikhism). Each of the broad traditions shares within itself local similarities and sensibilities which provide common ground within its stream of spirituality but which also creates areas of distinct difference from the other two broad traditions.

## PRIMAL RELIGIOUS TRADITIONS

'Primal religion' is a term used to denote the type of religion most often found in pre-literate tribal societies. While tribal religions vary in practice and belief they share enough common ground to be grouped as sharing an essentially similar view of the world. Within primal societies the different aspects of such a society relate together in an organic, holistic worldview. No aspect of life can be seen in detachment from other beliefs and practices. A supernatural view of the world suffuses everything. To draw a distinction between the natural world and the spiritual world as western societies often do would make little sense. Religion is not a cultural option but rather the heart and breath of life. The world is understood through primarily relational and personal categories that cannot conceive of the world as an impersonal object to be manipulated, as in western rationalistic scientific thought. The cycle of life, birth and death, and forces of nature, such as illness and the weather, are related to through spiritual powers, whether they be spirits, ancestors or gods. Christian theologian Keith Ward remarks that the implicit belief of much primal religion is that …

> 'sensory reality is an appearance of an underlying suprasensory world whose character can be discerned by processes of mental purification and whose powers can be used for human well-being – fertility, good hunting, and health.'
>
> Keith Ward, *Religion and Revelation* (Oxford University Press, 1994, p. 67)

In terms of mediating between the suprasensory realm and members of the community the role of a shaman, or holy man, is important in primal societies. The shaman acts as an intermediary or medium between the everyday world and the spirit world and as such provides the means through which the favour of spiritual powers may be gained or harmony restored in times of suffering. The suprasensory order is disclosed through dreams, ecstatic visions or through travel in the spiritual world while the shaman is in a trance like state in this reality. Shamans therefore act as vehicles of revelation to the wider population. As providers of access to the sacred they also serve to legitimise and reinforce the social structures and values already existing within their particular primal society. The source of religious authority within primal religions is also therefore located with the shamans.

## ARE RELIGIOUS TRADITIONS A DEVELOPMENT FROM PRIMITIVE ERROR?

Primal religions can be seen to predate all the canonical world religions and to have influenced many of them. It is arguable for example that the expanding religious vision that became Judaism arose out of the ancient Middle Eastern tribal religion of the Israelites as it rejected many of the traits of primal religion found for example, in Canaanite religion. Hinduism arguably has its historical origins rooted in the Indus Valley civilisation of North West India, about 4500 years ago. To recognise that canonical religions have been influenced in their development by earlier primal religious traditions has sometimes been taken as supporting an historical explanation of religion. Indeed, Victorian anthropologists such as E. Tylor and J. Frazer sought to explain religion through unearthing its historical origins and linking its subsequent evolution to a process reminiscent of the evolutionary theory of Charles Darwin (1809-1882). The atheistic philosopher David Hume (1711-1776) first suggested in his book *The Natural History of Religion* a rational naturalistic schema through which religion might be understood. He suggested that the earliest forms of religion were polytheistic and thus involved the worship of many gods. That many gods were worshiped arose out of a desire to deal with fear occasioned by the challenges of life, death and its many uncertainties such as illness and natural disasters. By worshipping the gods it was hoped that favour with the gods, and the weather and seas that they controlled, might be secured and life and family protected. Such primitive humanity gradually imbued the gods with more personal attributes and finally chose one of the pantheon of gods to underwrite the existence of everything else, thus leading to monotheism, the worship of one God. Such a perspective excludes the possibility of transcendent powers or the existence of God from the outset. Within such a perspective religion is seen as a mistake as humanity grew through the ages to reject magic as false it must now reject religion and embrace the age of science.

However, to acknowledge the influence of primal religions upon canonical religious traditions does not, of necessity, entail such a naturalistic, historical explanation of religion. To discern historical processes and relationships does not commit one to such an atheistic perspective unless you are already committed to a reductionist view of religion which excludes the possibility of the miraculous and the supernatural. If such a view is seen as attractive a serious problem remains, for it is impossible to prove that such an explanation corresponds to the origin of religion. We just don't have access to that kind of historical evidence as the British anthropologist Evans-Pritchard argued in the 1930s. The idea remains at the level of theory, and as a theory it also commits an error of logic known as the 'genetic fallacy'. This fallacy occurs whenever it is assumed that in explaining the origins of something you have shown its falsity or truth. A general theology of revelation, such as outlined earlier, affirms the possibility that revelation of the ultimate reality may be discerned through a process of human engagement with the world. That knowledge of ultimate realities might develop through time does not invalidate earlier perspectives as stages on the spiritual quest of humanity for Truth or spiritual wisdom. And unless a reductionist perspective is assumed the possibility of specific revelation through which God, or that which is ultimate, reveals itself through particular historical events or people remains.

## SEMITIC RELIGIOUS TRADITIONS

Semitic religions share a common heritage back to the patriarch Abraham and the role of prophets developed by the Hebrews. Semitic religions mark a break with primal religions as the Hebrew prophets of ancient Israel claimed to possess a clear sense of knowing the will of God. The prophets championed belief in a creator God who had a clear moral purpose for humanity and who would act as both judge and saviour of humanity from a fallen, sinful world. Such a prophetic tradition went beyond the localised powers and spirits of shamanistic primal religions to proclaim a universal truth about reality which rejected the human sacrifice, ritual prostitution and reliance on magic of ancient near eastern fertility religions, such as Canaanite religion. Yet, some shamanistic practices can still be witnessed in the lives of figures such as the first King of the Israelites, Saul, when prophetic revelations are gained through prolonged ecstatic, trance like, states. Such shamanism fades into the background as the tradition of Hebrew prophecy develops. Instead the prophets often called people to live within the truth of an earlier historical revelation such as, within Judaism, the Exodus event and the giving of the law as the Mosaic covenant between God and his chosen people. In as much as they upheld the ancient histories and revelations they were judged to be acting as agents of divine authority and blessing. The prophets proclaimed the existence of a personal God who as Lord of all was alone worthy of worship. Hence Semitic religions have within them a tendency to exclusivism which sees the true revelation of God found only, or mainly, within its own particular religious tradition. Keith Ward remarks that Semitic religions as

> 'prophetic religion stands for the transcendence of personal, ethical, and individual life, over against the

> reduction of human personhood to the rhythms of time and nature, and the ritual control of fate and fertility which the nature religions seemed to stress.'

*Religion and Revelation* (Oxford University Press, 1994, p. 102)

Within the Semitic religious traditions of Judaism, Christianity and Islam revelation is disclosed through historical events. Judaism would appeal to the giving of the Torah to Moses and the ministry of the prophets of ancient Israel, Christianity to the incarnation of the divine in the life of Jesus, and Islam to the imparting to Muhammad of the eternal pre-existent words now contained in the Qur'an. Each religious tradition holds within it a strong notion of the purposeful action of God toward the world moving his creation toward some future consummation. Within Semitic traditions God has created an ordered and good creation tainted by human sin and rebellion against God. Each tradition claims different means of resolving the disordered relationships between humanity and God. Judaism is mainly concerned with living the ethical life toward God and others, Christianity with appropriating the salvific value of Jesus, and Islam with submission to the will of God. Within the traditions there is a respective concern for the way in which the lives of Moses, Jesus and Muhammad disclose the divine law and commands. Within Semitic world views miracles can be seen as events through which God acts to direct creation toward its end goal and the overcoming of evil. The way of healing for the world and our lives is located externally to the world in a God who has existed eternally and created the world as distinct from himself. Such a monotheistic God is to be related to primarily through prayer that those who acknowledge the existence of God may foster a life of loving devotion to God and his will.

Semitic world views can be seen as involving the ongoing persuasive influence of God toward humanity. Revelation is primarily about encountering God or his will, whether originating in experience or the written word of holy texts, and formulating a personal response to that encounter. The idea of revelation as propositional has traditionally played a greater part in Semitic religious traditions than the non-propositional perspective through the Semitic concern that God conveys information to human beings through speaking, through verbal and personal modes of communication which establish objective truths.

## INDIAN RELIGIOUS TRADITIONS

In contrast to the Semitic religious traditions focus on revelation as encounter with God, Indian religions function with a view of revelation described by Keith Ward in his book *Religion and Revelation* as enlightened apprehension.

Whereas Semitic religions are primarily prophetic, Indian religions are mystical. While Semitic religion focuses on the external words of a creator God, Indian religions focus on the inner experience of skilled holy men who through meditation gain access to the suprasensory realm and an awareness of its cycles of existence. Through meditation, rather than prayer, trained individuals are able to know or sense the universal Cosmic law which binds everything in the universe together and hence become enlightened. The notion of Dharma, which puts in propositional form knowledge of the nature of reality and the means by which humanity may fulfil its duty or role within the scheme of things encourages conformity to the Cosmic law. The nature of the universe in Indian religions is immersed in the idea of Samsara, of a cycle of rebirth, through which the end spiritual goal for every soul is to seek unity of being with the ultimate reality. Such unity is sought by removing desire and ignorance which encourage an illusory perception of the self as standing individually detached from the rest of reality. In a context in which it is asserted that everything that exists has an impermanent existence it is asserted that an ascetic path to spirituality, which forsakes material possessions and concerns with worldly status, brings about a state of non-attachment toward things which opens the way through which bliss and contentment may finally be experienced.

There is no creator God standing apart from the world within Indian religions and thus monotheism is rejected. Hinduism has strong traits of pantheism within it. Pantheism states that the universe and God are one and the same; they are ways of describing the same reality. Buddhism is monistic, which means it rejects any idea that the ultimate reality is divine but believes in the underlying unity of everything that exists. Thus Indian religions are often characterised by non-dualism, which once again, stands in contrast to the dualistic nature of Semitic religions which stress the separate and distinct natures of the universe and God. While within Hinduism personal understandings of divinity may be seen in Avatars they are not the fundamental reality, rather Avatars act as special manifestations or vehicles through which the deeper ultimate reality can be glimpsed. This ultimate reality is beyond distinctions between personal and non-personal which again is different from Semitic religions in their stress on ultimate reality being grounded in the personal nature of God as a willing, relating, speaking Being. Whereas Semitic religions emphasise the importance of the activity of God in historical events as the source of revelation, Indian religions stress the importance of non-activity and passivity through the experience of meditation as the source of revelation. Miracles become the outworking of psychic powers in gifted spiritual holy men who are in tune with the suprasensory ultimate reality. The chief mode of revelation within Indian religions is therefore non-propositional. We have then in Semitic and Indian religions two very different, almost opposite, views of revelation.

# HOW HAVE SACRED TEXTS DEVELOPED AS RECOGNISED BODIES OF SCRIPTURE?

## THE FORMATION AND INSPIRATION OF CANON

In order to illustrate the formation of scripture as canon from both a Semitic and Indian religious perspective this section will focus on Christianity, Islam and Hinduism. The development of the canon focuses on the emerging agreement over time of what texts a religious tradition came to accept as divinely inspired, and therefore authoritative in matters of belief and practice for the community.

Keith Ward in his book *Religion and Revelation* (pages 218-219) suggests that the formation of canonical writings passes through four main stages. The first, which he calls the stage of primary experience, involves the prophets or holy men reflecting on their own religious experiences and its relevance to themselves and their society, as they strive to discern the will of the divine. The second stage, of primary witness, involves the preservation of the visions, prayers and teachings of the prophets and holy men through members of the community committing them to memory or writing them down. Thirdly, the stage of theological redaction involves members of the community evolving religious rites, festivals, creeds and traditions which seek to encourage participation and commitment to the wisdom of the prophets and holy men. Finally, the fourth stage, which is called the stage of canonical definition, is the point at which the religious community identifies a core set of truths which are key to the very identity of the religious tradition and the way it views life and the world. Such teachings and stories are seen as essential and given a special authority over the life of the community whether preserved in written or oral form. While historical questions remain over whether religious traditions actually form this way, it is useful to keep the schema presented by Ward in mind as we consider the formation of canon in Christianity, Islam and Hinduism.

## CHRISTIANITY AND THE OLD TESTAMENT

Christianity has its roots within the Jewish religion. The holy book of Christians, the Bible, is split into two parts: the Old and New Testament. While the New Testament focuses on the life and teachings of Jesus and the early Church, the Old Testament is made up of ancient Jewish scriptures that focus on the laws, history and relationship between God and his chosen people the Jews. The Torah, the first five books of the Hebrew scriptures, had taken the organised written form they now possess, rather than relying on oral tradition and isolated texts, from around 540 BCE as the Jews sought to reconsolidate their religious and communal identity following the return from exile in Babylon. The books of the prophets were added to the emerging canon during the post-exilic period between 300 BCE and the arrival of Christianity in the first century CE. In deciding which books to include in the Hebrew Bible a judgement was made on how well a given book fitted with the already accepted teachings and sensibilities of the Torah, and whether it was accepted by the community at large that a given text had been prophetically inspired. Given that post-exilic Judaism (after 500 BCE) largely believed that the divine inspiration of prophets had ceased with the return from Babylon this meant that only texts written up to this time were seen as inspired. The last prophetic writing to make it into the Hebrew canon was therefore the book of Malachi. The Jewish Biblical canon was effectively closed circa. 90 CE through discussions held at Jabneh, in Palestine, by leading Pharisaic scholars. While Pharisaic Judaism went on to compose other writings from earlier oral traditions in the form of the Mishnah, and in turn, record discussions over how the Mishnah was to be interpreted in the Talmud, these fall outside of the orbit of Christianity.

The importance of this discussion for Christianity is that it illustrates both the immense period of time over which the Hebrew Bible came into existence and serves as a reminder that at the time of the early Church Judaism was still at a stage of debate over the make up of the Jewish canon beyond the first five books of the Torah. Indeed, this is even more so as Jews living outside of Israel often read, as scripture, a Greek translation of the Torah and the Prophets which also included other post-exilic writings such as 1 and 2 Maccabees and Ecclesiasticus. This Greek Jewish Bible was written in the 1st or 2nd century BCE in Egypt and was called the Septuagint. Debates within Judaism over whether the Hebrew Bible or the Septuagint was authoritative led the early Church Fathers to draw the boundaries of Jewish scripture differently. The effects of this are clearly present within the form the Bible takes today within Protestant and Catholic Christianity. Protestantism, as James Thrower remarks in his book *Religion: The Classical Theories*, followed the decision of Saint Jerome (342-419 CE) to relegate the post-exilic writings included in the Septuagint to the status of important but not divinely inspired writings, thus following the example set by the Jewish Hebrew Bible. If Protestant Bibles have post-exilic literature at all it is included in an appendix called an Apocrypha. Catholicism re-affirmed at the Council of Trent (1545-1563 CE), in response to the Protestant reformation, a decision to accept as inspired the post-exilic literature contained in the Septuagint. In doing so the Catholic Church supported the view of the early Church father Saint Augustine (354-430 CE) and also sought to continue validating the role such literature had already played in Christian liturgy throughout the centuries.

## CHRISTIANITY AND THE NEW TESTAMENT

The early Church was, in the first instance a messianic movement within Judaism, which believed that Jesus was the Messiah many Jews had been expecting. The Messiah would bring salvation for God's chosen people and establish God's kingdom on Earth. That only a minority of Jews accepted Jesus as Messiah while the evangelistic ministry of the apostle Paul to non-Jews met with success gradually led to the early Church becoming a primarily gentile rather than Jewish movement. Alongside such a shift the early Church, which had often met in Synagogues, found itself increasingly estranged from Judaism.

Much of the New Testament is made up of the letters of the apostle Paul to Christian communities he had founded within what we now call Turkey and Greece. Other apostolic writings like 1 Peter existed and alongside the letters of Paul were treasured by the early Church as they preserved the witness of the disciples and apostles to Jesus. As Paul died in Rome in 64 CE letters that are ascribed to his hand such as 1 Thessalonians had to have been written before this date. Indeed, many scholars believe 1 Thessalonians is one of the earliest New Testament documents we have and that it was written around 50 CE. During the period between the death of Jesus in about 30 CE and the writing of such texts the early Church relied on other documents that have been lost in antiquity and oral tradition. Unlike relying on word of mouth today, in the ancient world the ability to pass on spoken traditions was skilled and accurate – as anthropologists studying pre-modern cultures still existing today have confirmed. During the first century most scholars agree that the four Gospels we have in the New Testament, Matthew, Mark, Luke and John were written. Scholars dispute the order in which they were written and exactly when but it is significant that the early Church came to see these four Gospels and the other New Testament documents as authoritative witnesses to the life and significance of Jesus. From other early documents dated around 150 CE we know that the Gospels were often read during acts of worship (Justin Martyr, *I Apology* 66).

The establishment of a Christian canon of scripture came about from perhaps four identifiable and related factors. Firstly, there was a growing need to establish a set body of literature as authoritative in order to combat heretical sects who claimed to possess secret knowledge about Jesus or the means to salvation. Secondly, although through the first three centuries of the Church there was a profusion of other writings being written by the Christian community, such as, The Shepherd of Hermas, The Didache, The Gospel of Philip, and the first epistle of Clement to the Corinthians, it gradually became accepted that there was a core group of texts which all the churches valued. Thirdly in establishing the early creeds, statements of faith, of the Church such as the Nicene Creed in 325 CE and the Chalcedonian creed in 451 CE, theological reflection on a 'core' set of texts was encouraged. Finally, the adoption of Christianity as the religion of the Roman Empire by Constantine in 312 CE probably encouraged the trend toward identifying a specific body of scripture as inspired as agreement over a set New Testament canon allowed

Christianity to consolidate its credentials as a universal religion rather than being confined to the particularities of place and time. In any event, by 367 C.E. the Bishop Athanasius stated in a letter that the 27 books which are now in the New Testament were canonical, inspired and therefore official scripture. While debate over some books such as Hebrews and Revelation persisted for several centuries these too became widely accepted in time. Pope Damasus formally recognised what had become standard practice within the Church when he formally recognised the New Testament documents as canonical in 904 CE.

The early Church would have originally understood texts such as 2 Timothy 3:16, which states that all scripture is God inspired, as referring to the Hebrew Bible or the Septuagint. As the New Testament corpus developed the meaning of such a text was enlarged to include 2 Timothy itself and other New Testament documents. In deciding which texts to include in the canon two important principles were applied. Firstly, texts had to be widely respected by the community of faith. Secondly, only texts that were thought to have been written by apostles (the first disciples of Jesus and the first leaders of the early Church such as Peter and Paul) or had been given their blessing were deemed worthy of inclusion in the canon of scripture. Hence the Gospels of Matthew and John were accepted in their own right while the Gospel of Mark was accepted due to its authors association with Peter, while the Gospel of Luke and the book of Acts were accepted because of Luke's close friendship with Paul.

When considered as a whole we see in the development of the Bible as canon an acceptance of sacred text being translated and further redacted (shaped) by its various authors and translators. Hebrew, Greek and Aramaic are all used. As the French philosopher Paul Ricoeur pointed out in his essay 'The "Sacred" Text and the Community', the translation of the Old Testament from Hebrew to Greek in the Septuagint, and the translation of the New Testament from Greek to Latin by Jerome provide witness to the open-handed way the text is related to by the community of faith. The Bible has since undergone translation into many languages and even different idioms, as the English version of the New Testament called *The*

*Message* illustrates in often very pointed ways. The act of translation involves critical thought over the meaning of the text and its interpretation. In this way Christianity and Judaism incorporate within themselves a critical dialogue with the text which sets a limit on the way the text is sacred. It does not possess special status because of any inherent quality it possesses as scripture but rather, is recognised as canon because it speaks of God in a way the religious community has come to especially value. This stands in sharp contrast to the dominant perspective found within Islam toward the nature of the Qur'an as sacred text. It is to this we turn next.

## ISLAM AND THE NATURE OF THE HOLY QUR'AN

In contrast to the way both Judaism and Christianity relate to the Bible, the dominant religious traditions within Islam exclude the possibility of critical dialogue with the holy text. The Qur'an is seen as a once and for all completed text that must not be changed. To read the Qur'an in translation is not really to read the Qur'an. It can only be really engaged with through reading the Arabic text. Exclusion of the possibility of translation limits debates over interpretation and meaning and secures the Qur'an as a universal text which the entire Islamic community holds in common. In this sense Islam is a religion of the Book in a way which is not found in the mainstream of other religions. The Qur'an is made up of 114 chapters (surahs), which vary in length from three to 286 verses. The longest appear first in the Qur'an and the shortest last. Much of the text is written in poetic form.

The content of the Qur'an is understood to have been revealed to Muhammad by the Angel Gabriel. There is some discussion whether these revelations took place all in one night or were gradually revealed over the next twenty two years until Muhammad died in 632 CE. Muhammad, being illiterate, memorised the various sayings. Over time Muhammad passed on the content of these revelations to his followers who wrote them down. After Muhammad had died the revelations to Muhammad were collected and recorded in the Qur'an, which was compiled in its current form about twenty years after his death under the leadership of the third Caliph

Uthman. Caliph Uthman then had all other versions of the Qur'an destroyed to ensure unity across the Islamic community.

For most Muslims the Qur'an represents the eternal and unchanging Word of God made known to man. Muhammad is understood as a passive recipient of this revelation and as such, the Qur'an is not the product of Muhammad or reflections on his own personal experience. It is a book of God not man. However the book contains much about how humanity is to live in light of God's existence while continually stressing the utter transcendence of God over the created order. The Qur'an therefore directs attention to the need to submit to the eternal mystery that is God who has made himself known through the prophets of Judaism and Jesus before the definitive and final revelation of God's will for humanity given to Muhammad. Islam sees itself as the culmination and end point in the development of monotheism found across the Semitic religious traditions.

Islam then, through the Qur'an, exalts the written word to a uniquely authoritative status. Revelation is unquestionably bound up with the words of the written text of the holy book. Rooting revelation in such a textual way not only goes beyond the traditional approaches found in Judaism and Christianity but stands in marked contrast to the way Hinduism approaches sacred texts.

## ORAL TRADITION AND SACRED WORDS IN HINDUISM

Unlike Islam with its focus on sacred texts Hinduism stresses the role of the spoken rather than written word in transmitting revelation. Oral tradition stretches back to around 1500 - 2000 BCE to the arrival of the Aryans in north west India and the closing years of the Indus Valley civilisation from which much of what is now called Hinduism originates. The oldest and most important Hindu scriptures, the Vedas, scholars have suggested find completion in the $2^{nd}$ century BCE with the composition of the Upanishads. Indeed, the Rig Veda was not published in book form until the $19^{th}$ century by a western scholar studying Hinduism. For Hinduism, relying on a more non-propositional notion of revelation rooted in experience rather than history it was not seen as essential to record revelation in written form. Within Hinduism sacred traditions can be mainly observed serving two functions. The first is to convey ritual activities which enable holy men, or Brahmins, to relate and perhaps influence the Cosmic law and the underlying nature of reality. Secondly, to pass on knowledge of how the cycle of rebirth may be overcome by the individual. Such sacred knowledge was passed on from teacher to student through a highly developed practice of reciting and remembering in a continual line of succession.

There are two classes of sacred words recognised within Hinduism. The first is called *Sruti*, which means 'that which is heard', and the second is called *smriti*, which means 'that which is remembered'. The various content of *Sruti* is believed to have originated from revelations gained by sages in ancient times as they listened to the eternal sound or word. This revealing of the eternal was in turn passed on by the sages to gurus, teachers. *Sruti* contains the four Vedas which are the Rig Veda, the Yajur Veda, the Sama Veda and the Atharva Veda. These variously concern hymns of praise to the gods, instructions for chanting, the conduct of sacrificial rites and magical spells. The Vedas are themselves sub-divided into four layers of tradition. The first, called Samhitas, contains the words of worship. The second, the Brahmanas, provides a commentary on the meaning and use of the words of worship contained in the Samhitas. The third, called Aranyakas, and fourth, called Upanishads, focus on more philosophical questions and concern over the nature of reality and the cycle of existence.

The second class of sacred words in Hinduism, the *smriti*, are mostly written later than *Sruti* with the earliest parts of the tradition dating back to around 500 BCE. Although less sacred than Sruti, the smriti are often better known by members of the Hindu community. The 'remembered' content of the *smriti*, rather than being made up of revelations of the eternal word, are dependent on human construction and interpretation however admired its words may be. Thus *smriti* has a lower status than *Sruti*. Within the *smriti* may be found stories about the gods and goddesses in the Puranas, epics such as the Ramayana, and within the epic Mahabharata the Bhagavadgita or song of the lord disclosing revelations believed to have been given to Lord Krishna. Krishna, as an avatar of Vishnu, the Hindu God of preservation, is thought to have manifested through himself glimpses of the deeper primal order and underlying nature of the universe. With Hinduisms focus on the spoken word and meditative or ecstatic experiences revelation is primarily ongoing rather than fixed definitively in a past tradition such as in the holy scriptures of Christianity or other Semitic religions. This encourages a continual diversity within the Hindu tradition in which six major schools of thought can be identified: Sankhya, Nyaya, Vaisheshika, Yoga, Mimamsa and Vedantic Hinduism. All of the schools, despite their various differences in focus and viewpoints recognise that revelation shows a universe in a cyclical existence involving continual rebirth (samsara). All of the schools are also concerned with the way in which each human beings true self, their soul or Atman, relates to the ultimate reality, Brahman, which unites all things in itself.

From the above it is clear that for Hinduism the notion of sacred writings is in fact an alien one. In contrast to the focus on the recital of the spoken word in Hinduism, Islam is a truly scripture based religion with its focus on the Arabic text of the Qur'an. Christianity and Judaism, while written scripture is undoubtedly important, tend to operate at a more midway point between these two opposing stresses on the written or oral word as the definitive bearer of revelation. Within Christianity and Judaism preaching, speaking out the truth, has often exercised a powerful place in the worship and witness of the religious community. Such a focus arguably slowed down the perceived need to establish an accepted canon of scripture within Judaism and Christianity until it was felt prudent to do so because of other factors (e.g. to combat heresy, to provide cohesion to the community etc.). But how do these sacred sources of revelation relate to other sources of authority such as: founders, tradition, leaders, reason and experience?

# HOW DO SACRED TEXTS RELATE TO OTHER SOURCES OF AUTHORITY?

## HOW DO SACRED TEXTS RELATE TO OTHER SOURCES OF AUTHORITY?

The relationship between sacred texts and other sources of religious authority varies across and within religious traditions. We will briefly consider four other sources of religious authority below: founders, tradition, leaders, and finally, reason and experience. Obviously there is much that could be said here and the student of a particular religious tradition should use what is said below as a starting point to undertake further research appropriate to their needs. As a general comment it can be observed however that the more a religious tradition stresses a holy text as uniquely authoritative the less influence other sources of authority will play an overt part in the life of a religious believer - unless those sources of authority, i.e. leaders, also stress the unique status of the Holy Book. In considering reason and experience, at the end of the section, thought is given to what happens when reason and experience is prioritised over sacred text.

## FOUNDERS

Hinduism is unique among the six principal religions of the Semitic and Indian traditions as it cannot point to an historical personage as a 'founder' of that religion. The individual with which a religion originates, at least in historical terms, is seen as the person through which God's will is revealed, or in the Buddha's case, the suprasensory realm revealed. Sometimes such figures take on a totally unique role such as in the case of Jesus, as God incarnate, or Muhammad, as recipient of the literal words of God. In both religions it is believed God, as ultimate transcendent being, makes himself known to humanity. This provides their lives with an unmatched sacred quality found in no other human being. Both Christianity and Islam believe their 'founder' was without sin. Both

Jesus and Muhammad become the organising hubs to which religious beliefs, practice and traditions make appeal, given that knowledge of God and the means to salvation is revealed through them. They are truly, like Judaism, religions of revelation.

In other cases such as Siddhartha Gautama, his authority as the Buddha lies in his experience of achieving Nirvana rather than receiving revelation from God. The Buddha becomes authoritative not as the bearer of divine knowledge but as the one who points the way beyond the forces of desire, suffering and rebirth. In as much as the Buddha's experience of Nirvana is achievable by others, both before and after him, he serves a less unique role even while, in the current cycle of existence his life becomes an important source of spiritual insight for Buddhists.

## TRADITION

Tradition forms as the community of faith seek to preserve stories from the life of the founding figure, his teaching, and reflect on his spiritual significance for humanity and pass them on from one generation to the next. Tradition provides the religion with its stability and continuity over time. Often symbolic rituals are enacted which seek to remember key moments in the founders' life or his teachings. Within Christianity, the Stations of the Cross performed by Catholics during Holy week serves as an act of devotion focused on the crucifixion of Jesus. Worship services which incorporate Holy Communion symbolically represent the saving grace of Jesus' death to Christians and provide an opportunity for thanksgiving to God. Within Islam through Hajj, pilgrimage to Makkah, Muslims show their submission to God by suspending their normal lives and focusing totally on God as they visit holy places and complete various rituals over a series of days. Hajj and Holy Communion are aspects of religious tradition which take on their own central significance in the life of the community of faith alongside scripture.

Holy texts can contain within themselves references to older traditions, such as references throughout the Bible to the purity laws in the Old Testament book of Leviticus. Books originally written as reflections on Holy Books can themselves become part of Scripture through the processes involved in the formation of the Canon. For example, in chapter 1 verses 19-21 of the New Testament book 2 Peter it is asserted that scripture (originally a reference to Old Testament writings) is divinely inspired. In contrast to this Islam leaves little or no room for incorporating the development of tradition within the Qur'an itself due to the belief in its reception by Muhammad. However tradition in the form of Sunnah, the witness of Muhammad's life and example, and the hadith, the sayings of Muhammad, informs the way in which Muslim law and the Qur'an may be understood.

Tradition also holds within it the creeds of faith, such as the Nicene creed in Christianity or the Shahadah in Islam. Finally tradition is involved in maintaining the acceptable forms of worship within a given religion and preserving its liturgy, hymnology or prayers. In short, if holy books commonly provide access to the divine word, tradition is the air that the religious form of life breathes.

## LEADERS

Leaders often play a key role in passing on religious traditions to the next generation of believers and in offering advice and guidance to members of the faith community. Within some religions leaders play a more prominent role than in others. Within Hinduism a Guru can act as a revered teacher or guide to spiritual realities who is highly respected by sections of the community while holding no significance for others. Within Islam and Reform Judaism the Imam or Rabbi often acts as a pastor and teacher to the community but is not involved in maintaining organisational structures or fulfilling sacramental roles in the same way as one would find in Orthodox and Catholic forms of Christianity. Within these older branches of Christianity Church leadership is hierarchically structured between bishops, priests and deacons. Bishops are seen as the inheritors of apostolic authority in deciding matters of faith and oversee a group of churches within a given area. They will also be involved in sacramental duties such as marriage and Holy Communion but are also the only leaders allowed to confirm or ordain new members of the faith community. Priests will lead individual Churches under the authority of the local Bishop and administer the sacraments, special rites which mediate the grace of God. Deacons support the priests and can often be priests in training. Thus, in some religions the role assigned to leaders helps provide structure and lines of authority which produce cohesion to the organisation of the community of faith.

Within Catholic and Orthodox Christianity, and Orthodox Judaism, leaders are also given higher status as interpreters of the Biblical text for the community. They are therefore sources of spiritual guidance and inspiration as they help believers understand holy texts and learn how their teachings may be applied to life. Within Roman Catholicism the Pope as Bishop of Rome acts on the collective authority of the Bishops within the Church. The Pope is more properly seen in relation to other bishops as being first among equals. Teachings of the Pope issued to the Church, which are conveyed through special letters called encyclicals, are normally understood as authoritative and binding although not quite having the same infallible (without error) status accorded to the canon of scripture. Such Encyclicals often focus on contemporary issues not explicitly addressed by the Bible such as contraception. However, where interpretation of the scriptures is concerned the Catholic Church sees itself, through the ministry of its designated representatives, bishops and priests, as providing the most faithful understanding of scripture.

There is therefore a relationship between scripture as the inspired word of God and the Church as providing the correct means of understanding it. However, since the reformation Protestant Christianity has rejected the authority of hierarchical Church structures and the authority of the Pope and bishops in favour of emphasising the importance of the individual's conscience guided by the Holy Spirit in deciding matters of Biblical interpretation and its applications to life. For Protestants the Bible alone is often seen as the basis of faith not Church leaders or tradition.

## REASON AND EXPERIENCE

Within the Protestant movement of Christianity can be seen an emphasis on individual reason and experience rather than a reliance on tradition or leaders. When Martin Luther (1483-1546) challenged the authority of the Church he unwittingly launched a movement which coincided with a shift in western culture which eventually led to the European enlightenment of the 17th century. The enlightenment marked a period of scientific investigation, technological development, and a questioning of old assumptions and authorities, such as that of the Church, in favour of prioritising human reason over any claims to revealed truth which might be found in religion. Theologians and members of the faith community increasingly judged the validity of scripture and Church traditions according to how well they fitted their own experience or were validated by reason. Thus, members of the various faith communities in Europe became increasingly influenced by the values and judgements developed by enlightenment thought.

The German theologian Friedrich Schleiermacher (1768-1834) famously declared in *On Religion: Speeches to its Cultured Despisers* published in 1799 that God was primarily revealed not through the words of scripture but through the inner experience of individuals as a 'feeling of absolute dependence'. In proposing such a basis for Christian belief Schleiermacher was attempting to establish a foundation for religion that appealed to reason and experience rather than Church tradition or ecclesiastical authority. It was felt that such a move would defend theism against the criticisms of atheists. For Schleiermacher religion involved humanity's

> "becoming conscious of his own limitations, of the fortuitous nature of his life as his being runs its course and silently disappears in the Infinite."

Such a reworking of the basis of revelation and knowledge of God abandoned revelation as propositional in favour of a non-propositional perspective. In his writings Schleiermacher fails to make clear what view of God underlies the 'feeling of absolute dependence' beyond an appeal to that which is infinite. Yet the infinite can be interpreted in several ways: as monotheistic, pantheistic, panentheistic or even monistic.

To move beyond the bounds of monotheism is to leave historic Christianity behind. Indeed, the Twentieth century Christian theologian Paul Tillich advocates such a move when he suggests that no transcendent God exists. Instead what we call God is actually 'the ground of our being' or 'that which is of ultimate concern' to us as individuals. It is this that focuses our life energy and supplies 'the courage to be' and achieve our highest human potential. Such a redefining of religious belief illustrates a radical reinterpretation of Christian belief to coincide with modern ways of thinking which many within the Church reject. Not surprisingly, how far reason and experience should judge ancient tradition and be prioritised over the witness of scripture continues to be a theme of much debate within the Church. Many believers assert that reason and experience need to be judged in the light of the witness of scripture and the authority of the Church if Christianity is to stay faithful to God. In different ways other religions have also had to face similar challenges.

Within Judaism several kinds of response can be discerned. Orthodox Judaism continues to stress the importance of the Torah as the eternal word of God while seeking to apply it to life today, and as such, seeks greater continuity with the past in the face of modern challenges. Hasidic Jews, who originated as a revival movement within 18th century Poland started by Rabbi Israel Baal Shem Tov (1698-1760), stress along with Orthodox Jews the importance of ceremonial Jewish laws and customs (e.g. food and dress codes). However unlike orthodox Jews, they stress the importance of personal experience and joyous worship as a means to drawing closer to God. This has, arguably, at times been at the expense of a dedicated scholarship of the Torah in place of studying Kabbalah (Jewish mysticism). Such an emphasising of experience over the holy book echoes the enlightenment turn away from revealed words to religious experience. Other groups within Judaism, such as Reform Judaism, can be seen as reshaping their self-understanding and social practices in light of the challenge of modern thought. For example, ceremonial practices may be dispensed with in favour of stressing moral codes found within the Jewish tradition and its ancient writings. Women may no-longer be seen as having to exist within a patriarchal system, and they may be allowed to worship alongside men in the synagogue. The liberal Judaism of Claude

Montefiore (1858-1938) marks a radical divergence away from propositional revelation in the Torah by affirming that God is never known in a literal way but rather through internal feeling. Such an approach reinterprets the stories of Moses in terms of their moral expression rather than as literal historical happenings. Within this perspective the Torah is not to be understood as the revealed word of God and religious authority is moved away from the Holy text and instead placed in the individual conscience of each person. Thus, another enlightenment theme is stressed, that of personal autonomy.

Islam has made a more unified response to the challenges of the enlightenment than Judaism and Christianity. Due to its firm belief in the Qur'an as the propositional and eternal word of God Islam has side-stepped issues raised by the enlightenment by continually submitting reason and personal experience to the authority of the Qur'an. In so doing it has effectively ignored the issues raised for religious belief by the European enlightenment. The above discussion opens up a consideration of how holy books may be inspired and interpreted.

# HOW CAN SACRED REXTS BE INSPIRED AND INTERPRETED?

## FIVE APPROACHES TO THE INSPIRATION AND INTERPRETATION OF HOLY BOOKS

To consider the inspiration of Holy Books is to be concerned with how God has made his reality or will known. The basic meaning of the word inspiration is to 'breathe in'. It denotes a discussion of how God is understood to have been involved in the revelation and formation of holy texts. Beliefs about how holy texts reveal or preserve the 'word of God' have an important influence on how they are understood. While some approaches to the inspiration of scripture leave little room for interpretation of the texts other approaches leave much more leeway for debate. Five different models of inspiration and interpretation will be considered. These are: a literal perspective 'Divine Dictation Model'; a conservative perspective 'Divine Guidance Model'; a second conservative approach 'Divine Encounter Model'; a liberal perspective 'Revelation through History Model'; and finally, a second liberal approach termed 'Inner Experience Model.' It will be seen that literal and conservative approaches have more in common with Semitic religious traditions and propositional views of revelation. In contrast the liberal perspectives have more in common with Indian religious traditions and liberal theologians within the Semitic religions who prioritise a more non-propositional view of revelation. That said, much diversity of opinion exists within each of the religious traditions regarding how inspiration comes about and how significant as a guide to life holy texts are. The five models articulated below are, for the sake of simplicity, exemplified from theologians and biblical scholars working with the Christian tradition.

## LITERAL: DIVINE DICTATION MODEL

This approach assumes the existence of God as transcendent creator. It is characterised by a commitment to monotheism and to a strongly propositional view of revelation. In order to ensure the Divine origin of the Holy text it is believed that its human authors were literally given, word for word, the content of the Holy Book. Thus scripture is the word of God in a definitive way, which leaves little room for interpretation, for the text means what it says. Thus, when scientific theories of the origin of the universe clash with creation stories such as that found in Genesis, Science is in error not the Bible. It is argued that statements such as that in 2 Timothy 3:16 and 2 Peter 1:21 confirm the Divine origin of scripture which, being from God, therefore possesses inerrancy. Inerrancy is the assertion that all Scripture possesses absolute factual accuracy.

Within Christianity such a view of Biblical inspiration gained popularity in light of challenges to religious belief such as the theory of evolution and scholarly attempts to analyse Scripture through historical critical methods. Toward the end of the nineteenth century, in a world increasingly viewing truth as only being established when knowledge could be shown to be certain, American theologians like A. Hodge and B. B. Warfield developed the idea of the inerrancy of the Bible as a means of establishing that the truths of Scripture are a certain foundation for faith and belief in Jesus as saviour of the world.

Within Islam it is believed that Mohammad received the entire contents of the Qur'an, as the eternal word of Allah to humanity. The night on which these revelations began is referred to as the night of destiny by Muslims. The content of the Qur'an was in turn revealed by Mohammad to his followers over an extended period of time and written down by them. The Qur'an is considered to be the 'Word of God and nothing but the Word of God. In it is preserved the divine revelation, unalloyed by human interpolation of any kind, unaffected by any change or loss to the original' (statement by the Islamic Council of Europe, 1976).

## CONSERVATIVE 1: DIVINE GUIDANCE MODEL

This approach also commonly assumes an attachment to monotheism and its belief in a creator God wanting to communicate propositional truths about reality to human beings. Within this perspective the Holy Book is not seen as inerrant (without any factual error) but rather as infallible. Infallibility entails the belief that in matters of faith the Holy Book is without error and will not mislead those who trust in it as a source of divine revelation. This view is perhaps the oldest perspective of inspiration within Judaism and Christianity.

Within both Christianity and Judaism it is accepted that their canon of scripture formed over a long period of time and so entails a belief in the providential guidance of God during its formulation and completion. Inspiration is therefore seen as a two fold process in which God discloses the initial revelation which is then recorded by members of the community of faith. But then God also guides the process of canon formation to ensure true revelation is preserved and accorded the holy status it deserves.

Catholic Biblical scholar Paul J. Achtemeier, in his book *Inspiration and Authority* (1999) argues that the inspiration of scripture arises before it becomes formalised in the canon as Holy Scripture from a dialogue between the traditions of the community of faith, the demands of situations, and those who receive revelation in the first place or are responsible in preserving it.

Within such a perspective the Bible may contain minor factual inconsistencies or be coloured by the interests and concerns of those who had a hand in writing the Biblical texts. This is because the Holy Spirit ensured what needed to be revealed was made known without taking over the mind of the writers. Inspiration of scripture, rather than being located in the dictation of the spoken words of God directly into the minds of individuals, is situated in a creative process involving the continual promptings of God to those who would listen and reflect on God's activity toward the world.

## CONSERVATIVE 2: DIVINE ENCOUNTER MODEL

Christian theologians Karl Barth (1886-1968) and Rudolph Bultmann (1884-1976) had an immense impact on Twentieth century thought about the Biblical text. They both detach inspiration from the written text of scripture and see it as a human book. Instead, inspiration is located in the moment of encounter between the individual and God as they read scripture or hear it proclaimed through preaching. As such this perspective starts to see a shift from a propositional view of revelation to a non-propositional one as events become more significant than ideas in revealing God.

For Barth the Bible cannot be called the Word of God for being a human book it is not divinely inspired. The Bible is however a witness to the saving actions of God toward the world as recorded by the community of faith. When a believer reads the Bible through the eyes of faith they participate in an event which has inspirational qualities when God chooses to speak to that individual through those words, at that time. The Bible therefore acts as a precious resource for human reflections on the divine which, whether through reading it or preaching about its contents, opens our spirits to hear God's voice. Whether the Bible is literally true in every detail or not is irrelevant, what matters is that it stimulates an encounter with God. Due to this liberal Biblical scholarship with its various quests for the historical Jesus becomes irrelevant for the Christ of faith is not a product of history but a living presence. Thus for Barth God's word is an event in which we participate, is active as it reveals itself to us as we ponder the written or spoken words of faith, and it is primarily relational and dynamic rather than static or immutable.

Bultmann, like Barth, saw the Bible as a product of human reflections on God and Jesus which was not in itself inspired. Like Barth he also rejects the quest of liberal theologians to try and locate the Jesus of history through historical-critical method. Both Barth and Bultmann see such a project doomed to failure as ultimately there can be no going back behind the New Testament texts and the Jesus of faith they contain to the Jesus of history. However, unlike Barth, he saw inspiration primarily rooted in the activity of preaching. The Bible becomes a witness to the past preaching of the community of faith. In as much as such preaching reflected a pre-modern view of the universe which believed in a literal heaven and hell, demons, miracles and an after-life, it has content within it not helpful to the success of preaching in the modern, scientific world we live in today. Bultmann therefore undertook a program of demythologising the New Testament in which he sought to reinterpret the mythical aspects of the Bible such as the miracles of Jesus, belief in the resurrection and in the Second Coming of Jesus. These are secondary expressions of faith and not timeless claims to propositional truths. Influenced by existential philosophy Bultmann argued that it is through preaching that we are able to come to terms with dread and anxiety about life which frees us up to live authentically, to take courage in the face of our own mortality and act in the world rather than being dominated by it. To demythologise the Bible is to free the tradition of preaching it bears witness to from the cultural constraints of place and time. This allows the preaching activity of the Church to continue to bear a unique and saving witness to the reality of God's existence and the importance of the Christ of faith. Bultmann was able to declare that "The word of God is not some mysterious oracle, but a sober, factual account of a human life, of Jesus of Nazareth, possessing saving efficacy for man."

Both Barth and Bultmann, by understanding inspiration in terms of event, were able to side-step much of critical Biblical scholarship within the liberal tradition and its attempts to unmask the Jesus of history. For both such a quest becomes irrelevant as truth is revealed through experience in the here and now – not by analysing sacred texts and the past. However, both Barth and Bultmann strive in radically different directions when considering the content of Biblical faith, i.e. Jesus as actual resurrected Lord and a belief in the Second Coming.

## LIBERAL 1: REVELATION THROUGH HISTORY MODEL

Within this perspective the idea of inspiration as the 'breathing out', disclosure of, God through Holy texts or through a process of engagement with them is abandoned. Holy books are seen as fully human constructions. Revelation as propositional is replaced by a non-propositional focus on a growing awareness by humanity of the nature of ultimate reality as history progresses. Such a perspective has its origins in the thought of the European philosopher Georg Wilhelm Friedrich Hegel (1770-1831). He believed that religious texts, beliefs and practices are immature strivings to relate to a truth not yet fully grasped. For Hegel God is an all pervading ultimate reality which he calls the Absolute Spirit. As everything that exists is part of the Absolute Spirit human beings are particular and partial manifestations of the absolute Spirit fulfilling itself. The cognitive reflective powers of humanity, enables us to recognise the nature of ultimate reality as Absolute Spirit and through recognising our unity with it, to see reality as it really is. The Absolute Spirit finds its fulfilment by becoming self-aware through humanity. As Hegel strongly criticised pantheism, James Thrower has suggested in his book *Religion the Classical Theories* (1999) that Hegel's philosophy is best understood in terms of panentheism (p.87). Panentheism is the belief that the universe exists through its participation in God but that the totality of what God is extends beyond the universe. For Hegel the truth of Absolute Spirit and its self-realisation is literally revealed through history as historical developments in philosophy and religion are seen as stages in the evolution of the Spirit toward its fulfilment. Such a philosophy has been immensely influential on both secular thinkers like Karl Marx and many contemporary thinkers in both Christianity and Hinduism.

Such a perspective is radically inclusive toward different philosophies and religious traditions albeit reinterpreting their significance through the idea of the Absolute Spirit. Indian religious traditions, especially Advaita Vedanta Hinduism, finds common ground in the idea of an ultimate reality that pervades everything else, although it differs over the notion that such an ultimate reality might find fulfilment through human history. The world religions, with their holy texts, creeds and rituals may look to make radically different claims about reality but such a model attempts to unify them through being understood as joint strivings toward an awareness of the Absolute reality.

While not committing himself to Hegel's concept of God contemporary Christian theologian Keith Ward has as the backdrop to his theology an appreciation of Hegelian philosophy. Like Hegel he seeks to see the roots of spirituality being primarily God centred rather than Christ centred. He also argues that it is through history that humanity articulates a growing vision of what God is through a critical and reflective engagement with religion and the mystery of existence. Such a quest binds the religions together within a common purpose even as they differ in their forms of life and beliefs. This emphasis marks an important shift in focus from the particular and propositional to the universal and non-propositional and in doing so moves theology beyond the bounds of traditional understandings of Semitic religions.

## LIBERAL 2: INNER EXPERIENCE MODEL

This model has its primary basis in Indian religious traditions with their focus on inner experience. It is because of this that within Indian religions, especially Hinduism, sacred texts are secondary to sacred words – for the spoken word is nearer to the inner experience than any written word held within a book. A focus on such inner experience is, as we have already seen, not characteristic of Semitic religions. However, the Christian theologian Friedrich Schleiermacher (1768-1834) marks a shift in perspective that has encouraged some Christian theologians to articulate an understanding of revelation and its relation to Holy Books that is not too dissimilar from the Hindu tradition.

Schleiermacher can be credited as being the father of the liberal tradition within Christianity through his call to affirm the inner experience of a 'feeling of absolute dependence' as revelation of God. The Bible becomes an outcome of human reflections on personal inner experiences and their feeling for God. So also do other Holy Books from other religious traditions. For such feeling arises from the universal experience of humanity as it relates to the challenges and mystery of existence. The inner experience model allows Schleiermacher to affirm that all the historical, canonical religions articulate in their own way reflections on experience of the Divine. Notions of God inspiring writers of holy texts directly or guiding them are foreign to such a conception of how humanity should relate to and interpret the significance of Holy Books and the propositional statements they contain.

Although Schleiermacher maintained an emphasis on Christianity as being the most important witness to the Divine through the redeeming activity located in the life of Jesus other theologians following Schleiermacher's inward turn have not felt this to be necessary. John Hick (1922- ) surrenders any notion of Christianity having special privileged access to the Divine. Rather all religious experience and its culturally diverse expressions in beliefs and religious rites relates to the same underlying spiritual reality. Revelation as non-propositional is taken to exclude the possibility of propositional knowledge of the ultimate being. This is a truly pluralistic vision for religion and lies in stark contrast to the exclusivistic sensibilities of the literal and conservative perspectives.

# IN WHAT WAY DO HOLY BOOKS ACT AS A SOURCE OF INSPIRATION FOR FAITH AND PRACTICE

How each of the religious traditions relate to the three ultimate questions mentioned at the beginning of this book shapes its faith and practice. In answering the question what is the nature of ultimate reality the object of worship is stated. In considering how best to live life, criteria for social action and the basis for communal living are put forth. When affirming what the ultimate destiny of human life is, a desire to make this knowledge known to others is often, though not always, cultivated. Each of these three areas, worship, social action and evangelism is inspired by the stories and teachings found in each religious traditions' holy texts.

## INSPIRATION FOR WORSHIP

Religious understandings of the ultimate reality often call forth acts of worship. For the Semitic religions of Judaism, Christianity and Islam this leads to a belief in monotheism. God has eternally existed and created the universe out of his own free will not out of any necessity. Creation is thus distinct from God and not to be worshipped. Although Christianity differs from both Judaism and Islam in affirming the possibility of the Divine uniting with the created order through Jesus as the incarnate God-Man each of these religions has a strong view of the transcendence of God and the need for humanity to submit to God's will and guidance.

A first pre-requisite to living the God centered life is to worship God. To worship God involves a recognition of the sovereignty of God over human life. Each of these religions seeks therefore to frame life within such a declaration of faith. Both at birth and death each religion utters words which focus on God and his greatness. Within Islam, for example, as soon as a child is born the head of the family will take the baby in his arms and whisper the call to prayer in the right ear and then the command to rise and worship in the left ear.

In dying the forgiveness and blessing of both family and God is sought.

Within each of these Semitic faiths there are foundational creedal statements which provide a focus for other acts of worship and statements of belief. The *Shema* is a Jewish prayer which sums up belief in God and states, in part, "Hear O Israel, the Lord our God, the Lord is one. Love the Lord your God with all your soul and with all your strength" (Deuteronomy 6:4-5). Within Islam the *Shahada* states "There is no God but Allah and Muhammad is the Prophet of Allah." In Christianity the Lords prayer found in Matthew 6:9-13 declares the need to trust our lives into the hands of God.

Such a firm commitment to the reality of God has provided an organising structure for the rest of life. Rites of passage such as marriage and religious festivals often make reference to the Holy Book of the religion. Often the festivals themselves, such as the Jewish festival of Passover, have their origins in the recorded history of the Holy text. Thus, the Bible, the Torah and the Qur'an all provide information on the God who is worshipped and give a rich resource of prayers and stories spoken out or reflected on during acts of worship or spiritual devotion.

If the Semitic religions commonly understand worship to involve offering devotion to a transcendent being, Indian religious traditions tend to possess a greater diversity over the object of worship. Within Buddhism worship of a transcendent being is rejected and instead replaced by a concern to support and implement the religious practices that might enable a soul to move closer to nirvana. Hinduism as itself a cluster of different religious traditions contains a vast array of different religious practices and beliefs. While most Hindus do have some kind of a concept of a supreme being, Brahman, in which the existence of everything else is united, some Hindus while accepting the cycle of rebirth, samsara, reject the notion of any kind of higher Being binding the cosmos together. As a consequence there is a rich diversity within Hindu worship. Sometimes it takes a more atheistic sensibility and focuses solely on the need to break from the cycle of rebirth through meditation and aesthetic practices. More theistically minded members of the

Hindu tradition may worship one or more of the pantheon of gods as a means to seeking protection and favour in this life or the next. The Vedas although commonly recognised as sacred scripture contain within them a wealth of religious ideas and practices which inspire such diversity in religious devotional practices. Reverance to the gods is offered through the rite of puja which is a form of ceremonial worship. Puja involves repeatedly speaking 'Om' the most sacred sound in Hinduism and the recital of sacred texts, often in front of a shrine with pictures or statues of some of the gods. The representations of the god(s) will be decorated with flowers, offered food and washed as a means of symbolically reinforcing spiritual commitments.

## INSPIRATION FOR SOCIAL ACTION

Social action, a concern for the welfare of others, is an important strand within each of the different religious traditions. To focus on social action is to consider how ones life relates to the wider community. Arguably though, in as much as Semitic religions are dualistic while Indian religious traditions tend to be non-dualistic, the way this concern is manifested has important differences. Whereas non-dualism entails affirming the oneness of everything that exists, dualism involves affirming the transcendence and separateness of God from creation. Given this, the differences arise through different conceptions over what being human means, and how we as individuals relate to that which is ultimate reality. For instance, within Indian religions there is a commitment to the law of karma and the legacy of previous lives in setting down the dharma or duty for the life now being lived. When coupled to the cycle of rebirth and the notion that everything is united, or seeking unity with the underlying ultimate reality the importance of individual lives lived is lessened. Indeed, Indian religious traditions commonly reject the western notion of an individual self. This can give ethics arising from Indian religious traditions a more passive character than those arising from Semitic religious traditions.

Within Semitic religions there is arguably a greater social concern for individuals. For there is no eternal cycle of samsara through which to be reborn. Rather, after this life the individual will be resurrected to face the judgement of God at the end of days. This places much greater weight on the spiritual significance of this life. Judaism has often sought to emphasise actions more than doctrines, perhaps because being Jewish has often been seen primarily as a way of life not as a response to a set of propositional statements, assent to which, opens up the path to salvation. Within Islam Zakah, as one of the five pillars of Islam, is a duty performed by Muslims whereby 2.5% of ones yearly wealth is given to support the poor, evangelism or the needy. In giving this money Muslims are reminded that everything they possess is a gift from God. Similar practices exist in Judaism, were sharing ones material wealth is called tzedaka, and in Christianity, were giving a tenth of ones income to the Church is called tithing. Social action in Islam is guided by Islamic law, *Shari'ah*. Islamic law is derived from a consideration of the words of the Qur'an and the example provided by the life of the prophet Mohammad. Within Shi'ite Islam, and in contrast to Sunni Muslims, moral prescriptions may also be made by specially designated leaders/Ayatollah's. In Christianity social action is often inspired by the example of Christ who is seen as laying down his life for the salvation of others. Thus, Christians have often been encouraged to be involved in social causes, whether they be to do with education, health or the alleviation of poverty. Christianity looks back to both the ten commandments in Exodus chapter 20 and the golden rule of Jesus in Matthew chapter 22 verses 37-39 to love God with all ones heart and to love ones neighbour as one would want oneself to be loved.

## INSPIRATION FOR EVANGELISM

Evangelism involves the communication of the need for conversion to the beliefs and way of life of a given religion to others outside of the community of faith. This tends to be a characteristic of Semitic religions rather than Indian religions although each religious tradition seeks to pass on its wisdom to others.

Semitic religions have a strong view of the need for humanity to be saved by God because of human sin, rebellion against God. While Judaism mutes the push to evangelism through a belief that the rewards of being righteous are for everybody, Jew and non-Jew,

Christianity and Islam contain a strong drive to convert others to the faith. In Judaism while there is no agreed set of beliefs describing the process by which a Jew may be saved there is a rejection of sin and wilful disobedience against God's will. Christianity has traditionally affirmed the need for the individual to recognise Christ as their saviour as it is believed that it is through his life, death and resurrection that humanity's relationship with God is restored. Islam focuses on the need of the individual to submit to God, which involves recognising Mohammad as the supreme prophet and messenger of God's revelation to humanity, and be doers of good deeds so that we ready ourselves for the judgement of God.

Both Christianity and Orthodox Jews believe that the Messiah will usher in the final days through which God's rule on earth will be fully established. While Orthodox Jews believe this Messiah is still to come, Christianity asserts that Jesus is this Messiah who, having defeated death through the resurrection, will come again at the end of days to usher in the kingdom of God. Each of the Semitic religions articulates a belief in life after death. While in Judaism speculation about what this might involve is discouraged, Christianity and Islam contain within their Holy Books specific teaching about the end of days. In 1 Corinthians chapter 15, for example, Paul talks about the resurrected body being a spiritual body which is also like ours in that it has physical presence. Eschatology, a discussion of end time events, involves a recognition that those who have sought the righteousness of God in this life will be blessed in the next. This encourages a desire, especially within Christianity and Islam, to help others recognise the reality of God's existence that they too might be blessed in the next life and fulfil their God given potential in this life rather than fall under the judgement of God.

While Judaism contains a more inclusive attitude to the rest of humanity and its salvation, both Christianity and Islam have traditionally tied the fate of individuals to their response to the revelation of God. This revelation is witnessed to by their respective Holy Books and the confession of the community of faith concerning the authority of Jesus and Mohammad as bearers of Divine and saving truths. Thus the drive to evangelism is tied to the ultimate destiny of individual souls and a belief in how human nature is to be properly fulfilled.

Notions of evangelism are for the most part foreign to Indian religious traditions. Hinduism incorporates such a diversity in religious beliefs perhaps in part because of an underlying assumption running throughout Hindu spirituality that there are many paths to God. A commitment to a non-propositional view of revelation encourages an acceptance that when views about God conflict the differences may only be different ways through which the same ultimate Being is known. Throughout history this has provided Hinduism with an ability to adapt and absorb into itself different cultural emphases and worship practices. In other words Hinduism often adapts to local sensibilities rather than converting those of other religions to Hinduism. That said, more strident forms of Hinduism undoubtedly exist, and can be found especially strongly in some parts of India.

# WORKSHEET

SECTION 1: WHAT IS RELIGION?

1. Why might functional definitions of religion be a problem for theists?
2. Why is defining what religion is such a problem?
   What advantages does Eric Sharpe's definition of religion have?

SECTION 2: IS REVELATION POSSIBLE?

1. Why are revelation and reason seen as competing sources of knowledge?
2. How does a general theology of revelation seek to heal this divide?
3. What are the main characteristics of general and specific revelation?
4. Which view of revelation, propositional or non-propositional, makes most sense to you and why?

SECTION 3: HOW DO DIFFERENT RELIGIOUS TRADITIONS RELATE TO REVELATION?

1. Do you think religion can be explained by anthropology, psychology and sociology?
2. How have theists responded to the charge that religion continues primitive errors in belief?
3. Draw a grid and on it mark out the main characteristics of Semitic and Indian religions. With a highlighter mark out the key differences.

SECTION 4: HOW HAVE SACRED TEXTS DEVELOPED AS RECOGNISED BODIES OF SCRIPTURE?

1. According to Keith Ward what four stages are involved in the formation of canonical writings?
2. What issues encouraged the formation of the Christian canon?
3. How do Hinduism and Islam differ in their approach to sacred texts?
4. Why has the issue of the translation of holy texts encouraged a more critical dialogue with the writings of Christianity and Judaism than that found in Islam?

SECTION 5: HOW DO SACRED TEXTS RELATE TO OTHER SOURCES OF AUTHORITY?

1. In what key ways is the Buddha different to the founders of other world religions with regard divine knowledge?
2. Are sacred texts more important than other sources of authority? In what ways would different religious traditions differ in their answer to this question?
3. Is Schleiermacher right to base knowledge of God in the 'feeling of absolute dependence'? In what ways does this reorder the traditional relationship between sacred texts and revelation in Christianity?

SECTION 6: HOW CAN SACRED TEXTS BE INSPIRED AND INTERPRETED?

1. What does it mean when it is claimed that a sacred text is 'inspired'?
2. Draw a chart of the five models listing the major characteristics of each. Discuss and note down any strengths and weaknesses for each approach.
3. Which approach do you agree with most and why?
4. Do you have to choose between perspectives or is it possible to hold, say, two perspectives together, in some kind of critical dialogue?

SECTION 7: IN WHAT WAY DO HOLY BOOKS ACT AS A SOURCE OF INSPIRATION FOR FAITH AND PRACTICE?

1. What are the three ultimate questions and how do they relate to worship, social action and evangelism?
2. How have people of different religious traditions been inspired by their holy texts?
3. Investigate the life of a religious figure within any of the principal world religions focusing on how the religion has inspired them to acts of courage, self-sacrifice and compassion toward others.
4. If there is no God and revelation is a human construct would such 'acts of inspiration' still make sense?

# EXAM QUESTIONS

The reason why most people fail examinations at A level and above is because they write irrelevant information as opposed to inaccurate information. The plea of examiners is always "...answer the question asked...". However, students often regurgitate answers from questions set during their studies. Such model answers are used irrespective of the slant or emphasis in the exam question.

It is important that answers are planned before embarking on an essay. Not only does this allow a student to arrange material in a logical order but this also serves as an 'early warning system' showing whether they have sufficient knowledge to fully answer the question.

One useful method to aid keeping to the required material is to highlight key words and phrases in the question and ensure you refer back to them throughout your answer. Consider the following examples:

**Explain the nature and role of scripture or sacred writings as a source of authority for faith and practice.**

In answering this question you may refer to more than one religious tradition although you do not need to. However, do ensure ideas are exemplified with specific details of your chosen tradition(s), for making generalisations is never enough. In answering such a question various themes need to be addressed. The task word is 'explain' so avoid evaluating and stick to unpacking your knowledge and understanding. Such a question has two parts to it and you must address both.

Firstly, discuss the nature of scripture. How does the religion see its Holy Book, in what way is it understood as 'Word of God'? Is it seen as inspired by God, or is it a record of the spiritual wisdom of past holy men and their experiences? Explain what the term inspiration means. If considering Christianity you might include comment on the idea of infallibility and the verse 2 Timothy 3:16. If focusing on Islam get across the idea of the Qur'an as the eternal, indisputable word of God. Is scripture primarily related to in a propositional or non-propositional way? Is the holy text an outcome of prophetic activity or meditative and mystical experiences? Is the power of holy texts to convey revelation contained in them as the written or spoken word? You are not asked to compare and contrast perspectives, so avoid this. But thinking about the contrasts between Semitic and Indian religions before the examination should enable you to be more articulate about whichever tradition you choose to write about.

Secondly, discuss the role of scripture. Explain the kind of truth it is taken to reveal. Does it provide laws to follow given by God, or is it offering guidance which is more optional? How authoritative is it? Give an example or two of passages linked to moral behaviour. Maybe the injunction not to murder in the ten commandments. Gideon Bibles are often found in Hospitals and hotels and contain pages directing people to various verses depending on what life issues may be concerning the reader. Think of other examples appropriate to the religion you are writing about. In as much as scripture may provide testimony of the history of a religion it provides believers with a rootedness in the past which is often seen as conferring on scripture a special authority. Various religious rites have their origin and take their importance from the testimony of scripture. For example consider the practice of baptism in Christianity, or the command to go and make disciples at the end of the Gospel of Matthew. Such a witness to the past serves to root the traditions of the community in the holy book. The sayings it contains, if spoken or recorded by the 'founder' of the religion, often take on a special significance in the prayers and worship life of religious communities. Perhaps provide one or two brief examples of this. Many hymns sung in churches reflect the Psalms of the New Testament and show how the holy text has been used as an important resource in the development of liturgy. Scriptures also provide a focus for the development of doctrines and beliefs, such as the transcendence of God in Islam. Consider other important beliefs that arise from reflections on the scriptures and how such beliefs influence the religious community.

**"In religion today, the authority of religious leaders is more important than the authority of scripture"**

**Explain and assess this view.**

Some questions contain quotes before the question. Here you are directed to consider the quote. However, on other occasions you may find that the question stands on its own and does not directly refer to the quote. In such cases quotes act as a stimulus to thought, and illustrate the kind of material you might like to consider in your answer. In such cases you are free to ignore the quote and focus in a different way on the actual question asked. In the question given above the two task words are 'explain' and 'assess'. So you have to show knowledge and understanding in your answer, but must also remember to evaluate. As you write your answer seek to move toward a conclusion which answers the issue of whether leaders or scripture are more authoritative. In other words argue out both sides of the debate with examples from your chosen religion(s).

Consider the authority of scripture from two or three perspectives within the literal-conservative-liberal spectrum. How much has it been challenged by problems with reason and religious experience? Does this make the role of leaders more important today? Does the faith of the believer rely on the guidance of the leader or the witness of scripture? Or does the role of the 'founder' of the religion, witnessed to by scripture, mould the way leaders today should behave and what they can believe? In which case does the authority of leaders itself rest on the legitimacy of scripture? If so then how much of a reciprocal relationship between scripture and the authority of leaders exists, and what would the consequences be for leaders, if the authority of scripture was undermined due to problems of interpretation? Obviously the tone of your answer will move in quite different directions depending on whether you exemplify your answer from a religious tradition that sees scripture as propositional or non-propositional, and whether scripture or leaders are seen to have divine authority and closer access to revelation. Don't try to say everything, but do ensure you back up points you make with examples, references to theologians, religious thinkers, or on one or two occasions a short quote, maybe even from the scripture itself.

# FURTHER READING

*Inspiration and Authority: Nature and Function of Christian Scripture*
By Paul J. Achtemeier
(Peabody: Hendrickson Publishers, 1999)
Readability: ** Content: ###
This is a closely argued conservative response to debates over the inspiration of the Bible.

*Foundation for the Study of Religion*
By Libby Ahluwalia
(London: Hodder and Stoughton, 2001)
Readability: **** Content: ###
Chapter 5 includes a section on the inspiration and authority of the Bible. Other chapters often include comment on the sacred writings of the principal world religions.

*A Brief Theology of Revelation*
By Colin E. Gunton.
(Edinburgh: T & T Clark, 1995)
Readability: * Content: ###
Although solely focused on Christianity it has many insights worth making the effort to discover.

'The "Sacred" Text and the Community'
an essay in *Figuring the Sacred: Religion, Narrative and Imagination*
By Paul Ricoeur.
(Minneapolis: Fortress Press, 1995)
Readability: ** Content: ###
This is a compilation of Ricoeur's writings. The short essay titled 'The "Sacred" Text and the Community' (pp.68-72) is especially important to those who wish to take the issues discussed in this booklet further. It questions the whole notion of Sacred Text as a once and for all given body of literature, and considers whether such an understanding of sacred text is an invention of the post-reformation mind. It is also suggestive of the idea that proclamation through preaching is more fundamental to the Jewish and Christian traditions than a closed canon of holy text.

*The Universe Next Door*
By James W. Sire.
(Downers Grove: IVP, 1988)
Readability: **** Content: ###
It provides an analysis of different worldviews. Chapter 2 covers Christian theism, while chapter 7 considers Eastern Pantheistic Monism which is often associated with Indian religions. An excellent introductory book which helps put the discussion of revelation in a wider context. Various non-religious perspectives such as naturalism and nihilism are also discussed.

*The Authority of the Bible*
By William Strange.
(London: Darton, Longman and Todd, 2000)
Readability: **** Content: ###
This is an excellent introductory book to explore issues relating to the Bible. It is very readable and is sprinkled with exercises to help you reflect on the problems of scriptural authority and the nature of the Bible.

*Religion: The Classical Theories*
By James Thrower.
(Edinburgh: Edinburgh University Press, 1999)
Readability: *** Content: ###
The book discusses a wide range of theories on the nature of religion. Chapter 2 on the nature of revelation is especially instructive. Chapters 3 and 4 discussing the relationship between revelation and experience and philosophy are worth making the effort to read.

*Religion and Revelation: A Theology of Revelation in the World's Religions*
By Keith Ward.
(Oxford: Clarendon Press, 1994)
Readability: ** Content: ###
A demanding read but very informative analysis of the place and role of revelation in the principal world religions. Well worth dipping into.

| | | | |
|---|---|---|---|
| **KEY** | Readability | * manageable; | ** good; |
| | | *** very good; | **** excellent. |
| | Content | # adequate; | ## good; |
| | | ### very good; | #### excellent. |

# GLOSSARY

**Allegory** – representing an idea through linking it to another object or person. For example, in the parable of the prodigal son told by Jesus, the forgiving father is often understood to stand for God while the forgiven son stands for the repentant sinner.

**Apocrypha** – this is a collection of thirteen books which are included in the Septuagint (Greek translation of the Hebrew Bible). The Roman Catholic Church accepts the Apocrypha into the Bible while protestants do not.

**Atheism** – a belief that there is no God. Atheists do not necessarily think that they can prove atheism to be true.

**Biblical Literalism** – an approach to understanding the Bible which interprets the text at face value. For example, talk of six days of creation does in fact mean six 24 hour days. As the Bible is also believed to be the literal 'Word of God' what it says is the final authority in matters of faith, life and in our understanding of reality. Biblical literalism is often linked to fundamentalism.

**Creed** – This is a statement of what believers affirm as their core set of beliefs about the nature of God, reality or the means to attain enlightenment or salvation. Creeds are often used in worship and prayers.

**Demythologising** – The German theologian Rudolf Bultmann (1884-1976) argued that the Bible is best understood if mythical stories, such as the miracles of Jesus and talk of angels and demons, are understood as conveying subjective attitudes and feelings rather than as reports of historical events. He argued that a demythologised Bible would be more relevant to modern man, and therefore make God more accessible in a scientific age.

**Dualism** – As primarily used in this booklet it refers to the belief that the being of God stands separate from the rest of world. Semitic religions are dualistic while Indian religions tend more toward non-dualism and monism.

**European Enlightenment** – this refers to a movement emerging out of the seventeenth century which was critical of religious authority. Instead it stressed the need for each individual to think for themselves, and appealed to human reason and scientific methods as arbiters of truth rather than ecclesiastical authorities or holy texts.

**Exclusivism** – a belief that the truth, wisdom or God is uniquely found in one religious tradition to the exclusion of others.

**Fundamentalism** – is a wide-ranging movement spread across the different denominations of Christianity that supports biblical literalism alongside the notion that the Bible is without error. Fundamentalism is sometimes associated with movements in other religions which take a similar literalist view of their own holy books.

**General revelation** – the idea that the reality of the existence of God is pointed toward through, for example, the existence of the universe, its design and beauty. General revelation is open to everyone and not linked to a particular religious tradition. General revelation often leads to a concern for natural theology and arguments for the existence of God.

**Inclusivism** – the view that while a given religion may reveal God better than other religions, other religions still provide valuable spiritual insights.

**Indian Religions** – this refers to Hinduism, Buddhism and Sikhism. They are all influenced to varying degrees by the idea of samsara and the eternal cycle of rebirth.

**Inerrancy** – a belief that the holy book contains no errors. All statements of fact are correct. So, for example, when Genesis says the world was created in six days, this is true. An inerrantist view of scripture sees the holy book as without error on matters of science, theological doctrines and history.

**Infallibility** – this is a softer position than that taken by inerrancy above. While it is possible for historical or factual statements in scripture to be debated, the holy book will not fail as a spiritual guide. Scripture is seen as uniquely fit to fulfil the purpose for which it has come into being, and that is to guide and sustain people in a relationship with God.

**Inspiration** – a belief in the inspiration of a holy text denotes its divine origins in the mind or purposes of God. Inspiration often implies that God has given the words of the text to its human writers, or guided them to the truth as they were willing to respond to God's influence. Inspired scriptures are often spoken of as being the 'word of God'.

**Immanence** – a term often used to describe the presence of God, or the ultimate reality, in the world.

**Monism** – this term is applied to a diverse set of worldviews ranging across the spectrum from religions such as Buddhism to non-religious atheistic perspectives. It affirms that everything that exists is part of the same ultimate reality. Monism entails a strongly non-dualistic view of reality for all that exists, including human beings, who are particular manifestations of the same underlying essence that can be found in everything else.

**Monotheism** – belief in an all-powerful and transcendent God who created the universe.

**Objective** – a judgement concerning objects, with its truth and falsity being independent of what anyone thinks about the matter, e.g. 'Cows have udders'.

**Panentheism** – the world exists within God yet God also transcends, exists beyond, the world. The purposes and fulfillment of God and the world are closely tied together.

**Pantheism** – the belief that humanity and nature are elements of an all-inclusive divinity (God).

**Pluralism** – the idea that all religions are to be equally valued as vehicles through which God or the ultimate reality may be experienced or shown.

**Propositional statement** – these are statements which assert a claim about the way reality is.

**Realism** – a position which holds that truth is independent of our thinking about it, there is actually some 'real' fact of the matter. For example, the realist view of God is that there actually exists in reality some supernatural being.

**Semitic Religions** – these are Judaism, Christianity and Islam. Each of these religions can trace their origins to the patriarch Abraham and the Middle East. They all possess a strong commitment to monotheism and a linear view of history – God created the world and at some point in the future will bring it to some kind of confirmation, fulfilling end point.

**Specific revelation** – this is a form of revelation found in holy books and the religious experiences of people. It is specific because it has its origins in the particular dealings of God with a given individual or religious community.

**Subjective** – in philosophy if something is subjective it is personal to a given individual. As personal it is an inner experience or belief that may not be shared or provable to other people.

**Theism** – a belief in some supernatural agent, usually called God.

**Transcendence** – often used to refer to the existence of God beyond the created world.

**Worldview** – is a way of understanding and living in the world.